TAKE A CLOSER LOOK!

AN INTRODUCTION TO MICROSCOPES
for Young Scientists

TAKE A CLOSER LOOK!

AN INTRODUCTION TO MICROSCOPES
for Young Scientists

Published by
Heron Books, Inc.
20950 SW Rock Creek Road
Sheridan, OR 97378

heronbooks.com

Special thanks to all the teachers and students who provided feedback instrumental to this edition.

Fifth Edition © 1979, 2021 Heron Books.
All Rights Reserved

ISBN: 978-0-89-739240-2

Any unauthorized copying, translation, duplication or distribution, in whole or in part, by any means, including electronic copying, storage or transmission, is a violation of applicable laws.

The Heron Books name and the heron bird symbol are registered trademarks of Delphi Schools, Inc.

Printed in the USA

13 May 2021

At Heron Books, we think learning should be engaging and fun. It should be hands-on and allow students to move at their own pace.

To facilitate this we have created a learning guide that will help any student progress through this book, chapter by chapter, with confidence and interest.

Get learning guides at
heronbooks.com/learningguides.

For teacher resources,
such as a final exam, email
teacherresources@heronbooks.com.

We would love to hear from you!
Email us at *feedback@heronbooks.com.*

Your YOUNG SCIENTIST JOURNAL

Scientists love to explore the world and how things in it work. They like to go new places and discover things they've never seen before.

They also like to keep track of what they find. They often fill books with notes and drawings of what they see, and include their thoughts and questions about it. These books are called *science journals*.

What's fun about a science journal is that you can use it to draw pictures or sketches of things that interest you. You can write down ideas you have about things, make maps, write down questions you have and things you want to find out more about. You might even stick in it samples of things you find—flowers, bugs, leaves, feathers, spider's webs—who knows what?

The learning guide that goes with this book will sometimes ask you to look at things and make notes or drawings in a journal of your own.

Whatever you put in your science journal, it will be full of your own personal discoveries. No two journals are alike.

You can use a journal like the one shown here, or you can use a notebook of your choice. You might even want to make your own science journal and use that.

Whichever type of journal you choose, it will be a place to keep drawings and notes about what you are finding out about the world and how it works.

So get ahold of a science journal, or make one, and then get going to see what you can find out. Who knows what might be waiting for you?

IN THIS BOOK

1 BEING A SCIENTIST — 1
Tools Scientists Use — 3

2 THE MICROSCOPE — 7
How Does a Microscope Work? — 9

3 SLIDES — 11
Prepared Slides — 13

4 PARTS OF A MICROSCOPE — 15
Find the Parts of a Microscope — 19

5 SETTING UP A MICROSCOPE — 21
Set Up a Microscope — 25

6 LOOKING AT A SLIDE — 27
Look at a Slide — 31

7 MAKING YOUR OWN SLIDES — 33
Make Your Own Slide — 35

8 **DRAWING WHAT YOU SEE** 37
    Draw Powder 40
    Draw Salt 41
    Draw Sugar 42
    Draw Onion Skin 43
    Draw a Bug 44
    Draw a Feather 45
    Draw a Bug with Wings 46
    Draw Pond Water 47

9 **THE MICROSCOPIC WORLD** 49
    Draw a New Object 51

1

Scientists are people who observe things in the world around them. They study things, and they do this because they want to understand how things work.

One scientist, for example, might want to know why animals behave the way they do.

Another scientist might want to understand what makes plants grow.

Another might want to know all about electricity and how it can be used.

A different scientist might want to know how to make machines work. And how to make them work even better.

Or to understand how the human body works, and how to keep it healthy.

Another scientist might want to understand our planet Earth, and everything about it. They might want to understand other planets, the sun and stars.

There are so many things that scientists want to learn about and understand better that we can barely name them all.

How do scientists do this? It's actually pretty simple. They understand things by *looking* at them.

Think about it. You're a young scientist! How do *you* find out about things?

You do a lot of LOOKING! You LOOK and LOOK, and LOOK some more!

TOOLS SCIENTISTS USE

Over the years, scientists have discovered ways to look at things more closely. Being so curious, they have invented tools for doing this.

If you stop and think about it, you can probably come up with some tools that scientists have invented so they can observe better.

Here are a few examples.

Telescopes help them look more closely at distant stars and planets.

A stethoscope helps a doctor listen to your heartbeat. It helps someone OBSERVE, but this time using the sense of hearing.

Cameras of all kinds help scientists study things. A camera attached to a drone lets someone see what a part of the world looks like from up above. It helps them LOOK at it in a new way and understand it better.

Thermometers help people study the weather by OBSERVING the temperature.

Scientists who study earthquakes have tools for measuring how much the earth is shaking and for telling them exactly where an earthquake is. These tools help them LOOK at earthquakes more closely to understand them better.

Tools like these that scientists use for looking and observing are called instruments. An **instrument** is a special tool or piece of equipment for doing some job.

The instruments scientists use help them LOOK and OBSERVE more closely. They help them study things so they can understand them better.

Being a scientist is all about LOOKING.

2

A **microscope** is an instrument scientists use to look at things that are tiny. In fact, *microscope* is a word put together from *micro,* which means "very small" and *scope* which means "look at."

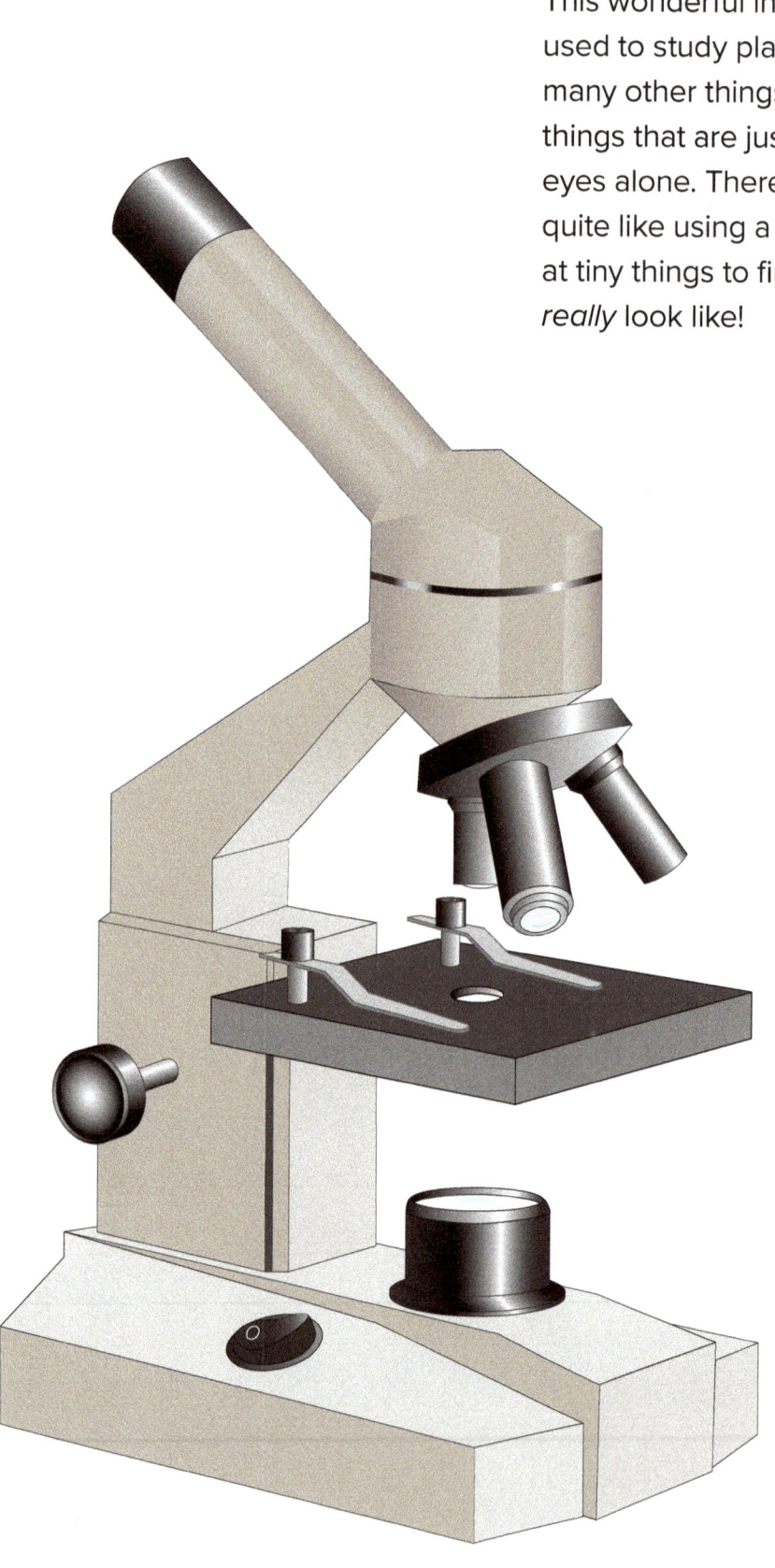

This wonderful instrument can be used to study plants, animals and many other things by letting you see things that are just too small for your eyes alone. There's actually nothing quite like using a microscope to look at tiny things to find out what they *really* look like!

HOW DOES A MICROSCOPE WORK?

A microscope is made up of several magnifying glasses. Each one of these is a piece of curved glass called a **lens**. A lens can make things look bigger, and when you put several lenses together inside a microscope, they can make things look *much* bigger.

So when you put something under a microscope and look at it, its very tiny parts look much larger and you will be able to see things you've never seen before!

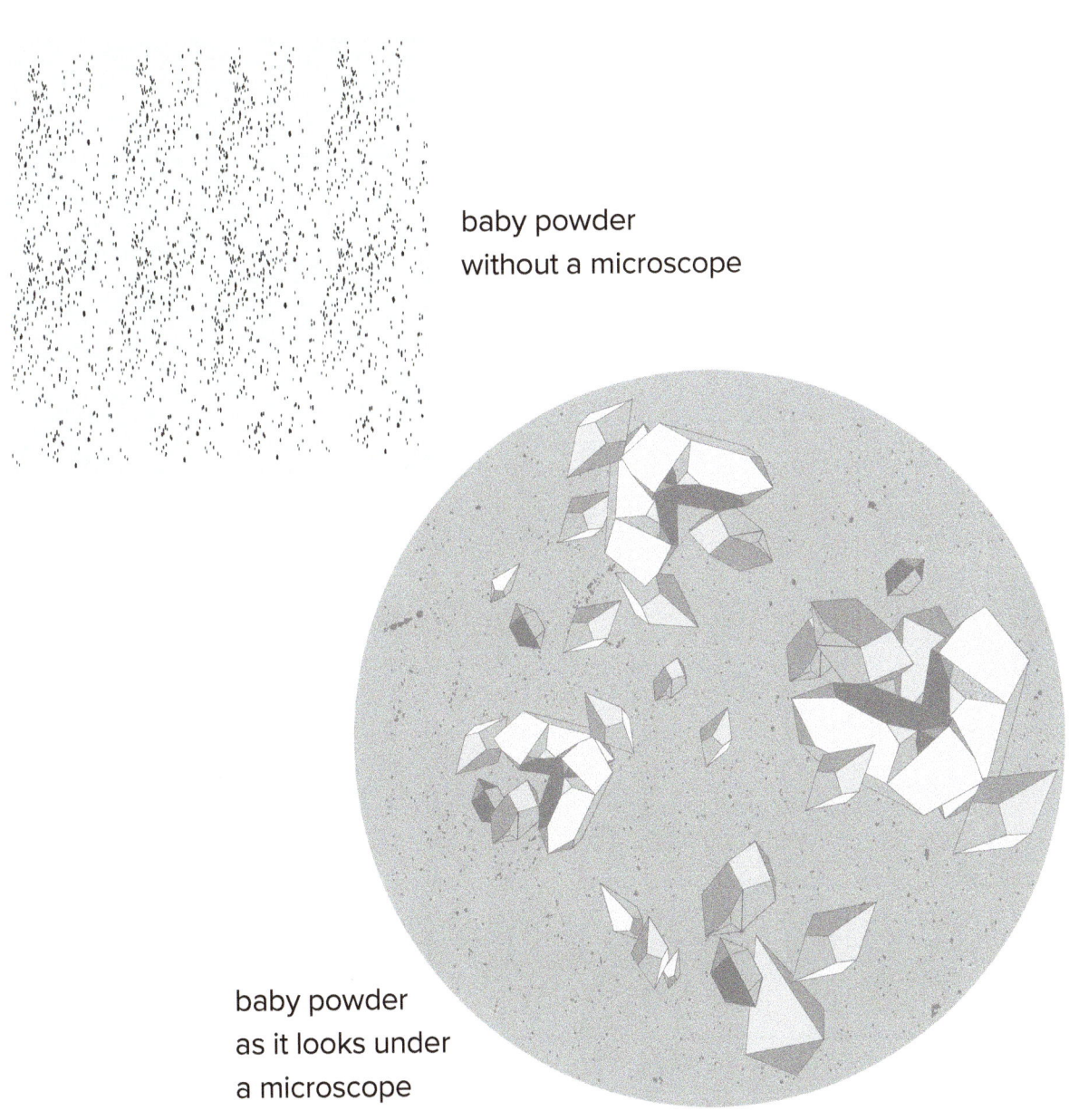

baby powder without a microscope

baby powder as it looks under a microscope

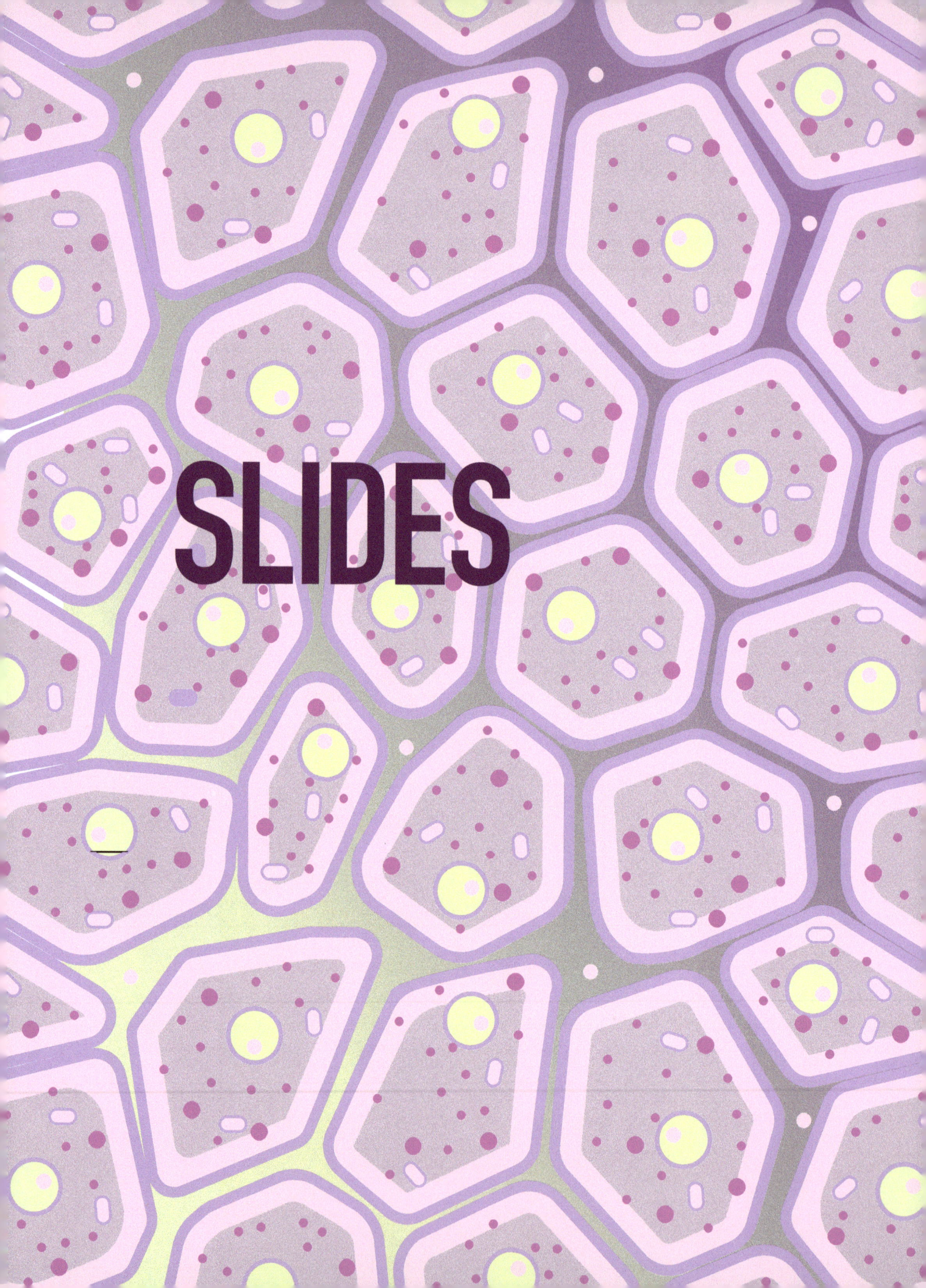

3

Here are some things you will want to know about when you begin to use a microscope.

Slide

A **slide** is a small rectangular piece of glass or clear plastic. When you want to look at something under a microscope, you first put it on a slide.

Cover slip

A **cover slip** is a thin, square piece of glass or clear plastic that you put on top of the slide. Together the slide and cover slip hold what you are going to look at nice and still.

PREPARED SLIDES

You can buy slides with things to look at already on them. These are called **prepared slides**.

The thing to look at is usually stained (colored) with ink so you can see it better. A cover slip is glued over it to protect it.

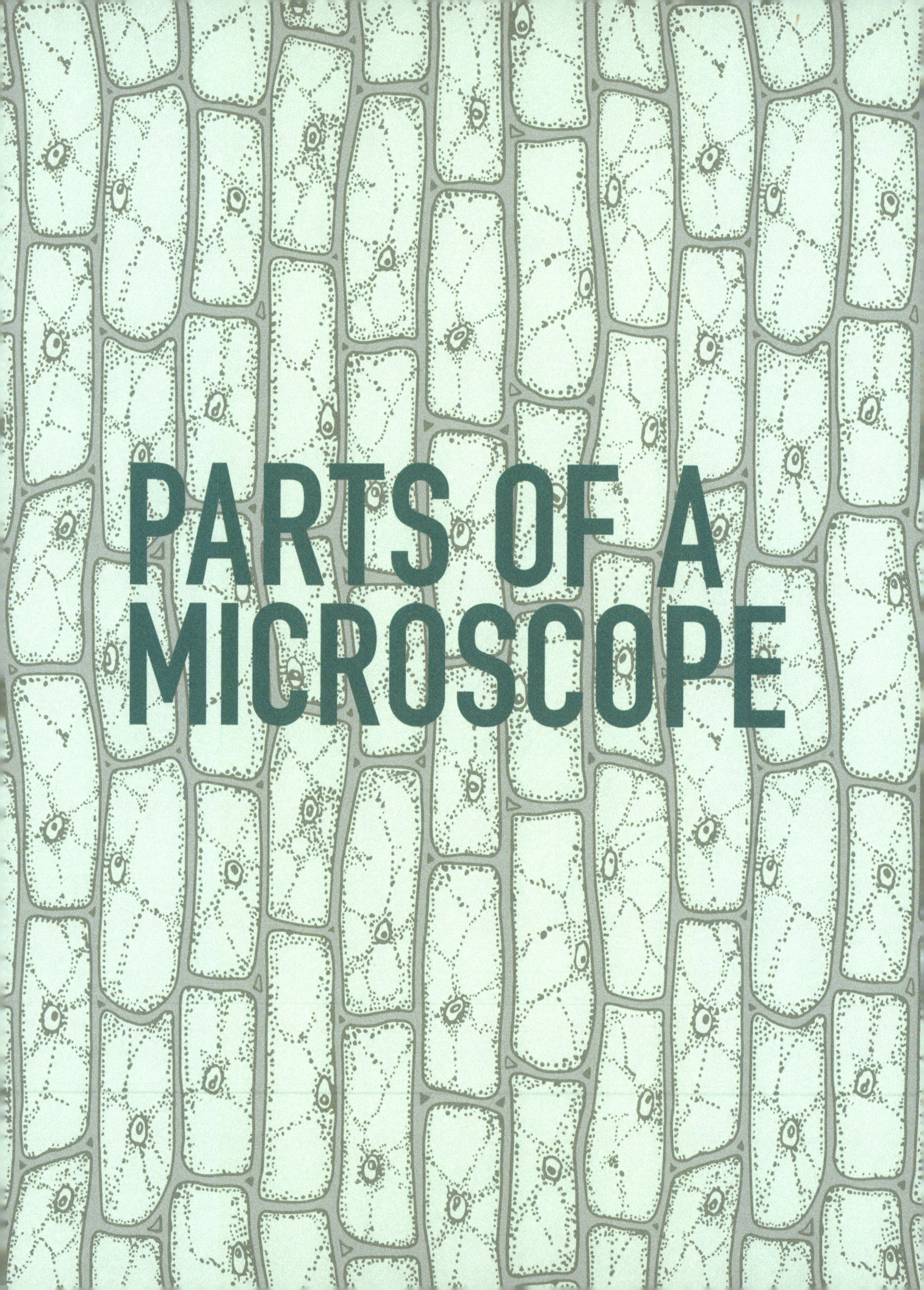

4

Let's learn the parts of a microscope!

Eyepiece

This is the part you look through. There is a lens here. Only two things should touch a lens: your breath and special lens paper. To clean the lens, breathe on it and wipe it gently with lens paper.

Rotating nosepiece

This turns to place different objective lenses above the object.

Objective lenses

These are different lenses that you set above the object you want to see.

Slide clips

These hold the slide on the stage.

Stage

The slide rests on it.

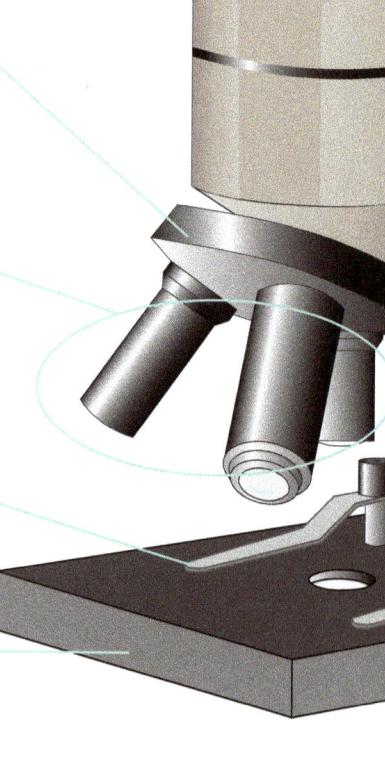

Light

This sends light up through the object.

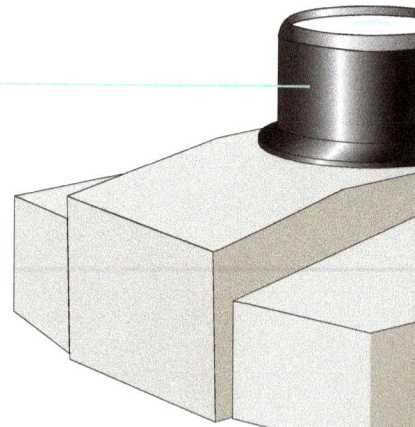

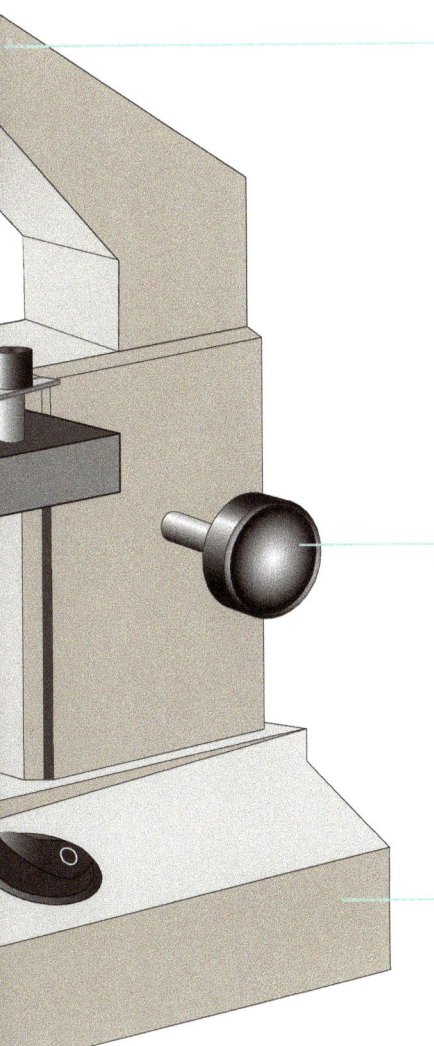

Barrel
This holds the lenses.

Handle
This is what you use to pick up the microscope.

Adjusting knob
This moves the stage up and down.

Base
This is what the microscope stands on.

FIND THE PARTS OF A MICROSCOPE

For this activity you will need

- An elementary microscope with three objective lenses

Steps

1. On a real microscope, find these parts:

   - barrel
   - objective lenses
   - rotating nosepiece
   - adjusting knob
   - stage
   - handle
   - light
   - slide clips
   - base

2. Have someone call off the microscope parts while you point them out until you can do this easily.

3. Have someone point to a part of the microscope. You say what it is and what it is for. Continue until you can do this easily.

SETTING UP A MICROSCOPE

5

To use a microscope to look at things, you need to know how to set it up.

To start with, get a microscope and a prepared slide. Then follow these easy steps.

1. Stand or sit behind the microscope so you can comfortably look through the eyepiece.

2. Turn on the microscope light.

3. Turn the rotating nosepiece so that the low-power lens is lined up with the barrel.

    > The **power** of a lens is how much it magnifies, or makes the object look larger. The smallest objective lens is low power, so it only magnifies a little. The next larger objective lens is medium power, and it magnifies more. The largest lens is high power, and it magnifies the most.

4. Turn the adjusting knob until there is plenty of room between the stage and the objective lens. There should be enough space for you to get your hand between the lens and the stage. If there isn't enough room, you could damage the slide when you put it on.

5. Holding a slide by the edges (so you don't leave fingerprints), place it on the stage and center it over the light.

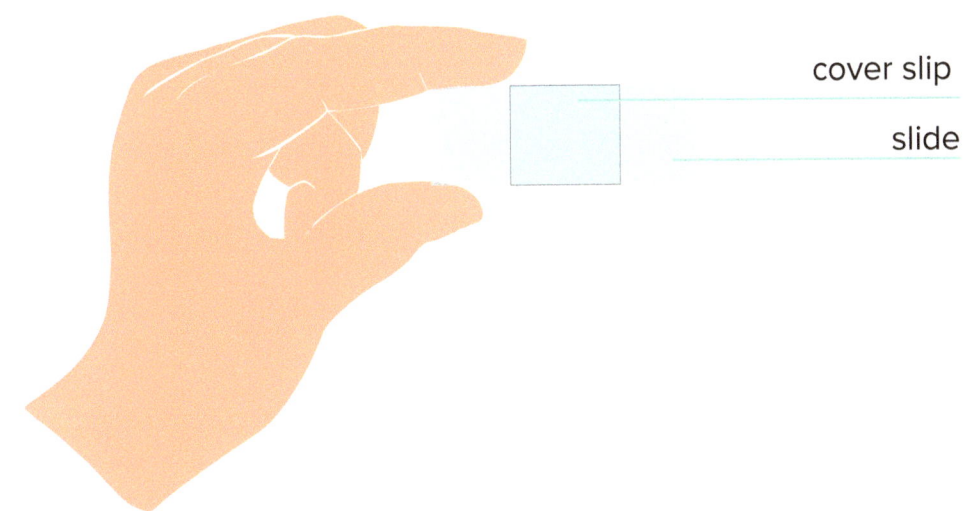

6. Clip the slide onto the stage with the slide clips so that it doesn't move around.

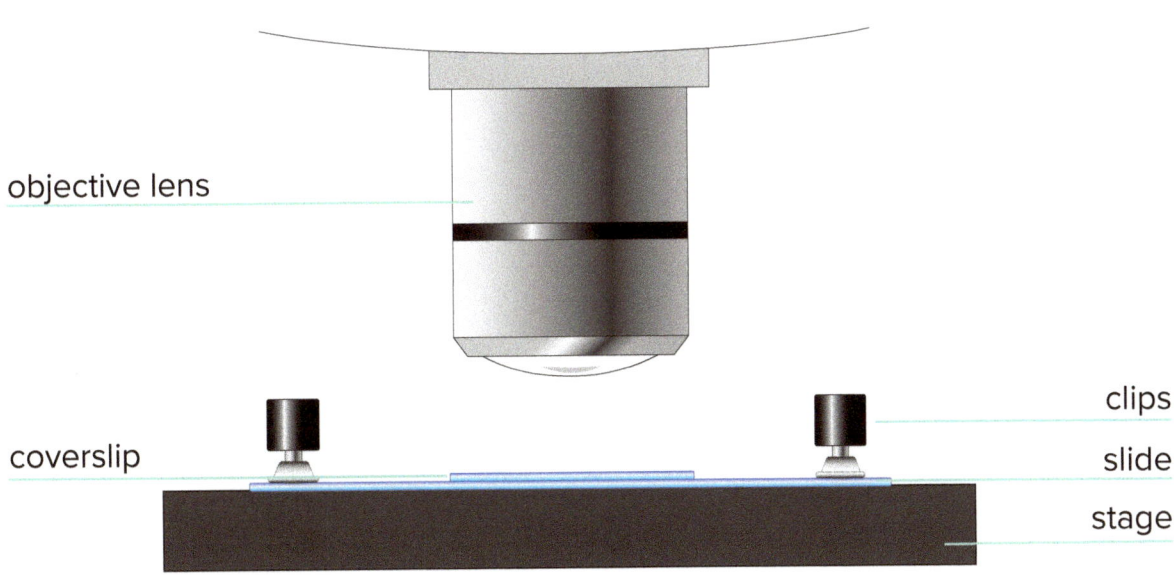

SET UP A MICROSCOPE

For this activity you will need

- an elementary microscope
- a prepared slide

Steps

1. With someone helping you, do each of the steps of setting up a microscope.

   1. Stand or sit behind the microscope so you can comfortably look through the eyepiece.
   2. Turn on the microscope light.
   3. Line up the low-power lens with the barrel.
   4. Turn the adjusting knob so there is room between the stage and the objective lens.
   5. Center the slide on the stage over the light.
   6. Clip the slide onto the stage.

2. Practice doing steps #2–6 over and over until you can set up a microscope easily.

LOOKING AT A SLIDE

6

When you look at a slide, you want what you're looking at to be clear and easy to see. This means you need to know how to **focus** your microscope. In other words, you need to know what to do to make what you're looking at very clear.

Here's how you focus your microscope.

1. Start by using the low-power lens because it is the easiest to use. Look through the eyepiece and turn the adjusting knob *slowly* so the stage and object get closer together. Do this until you can see the object clearly.

2. Next use the medium objective lens. Without moving the slide or the adjusting knob, rotate the nosepiece until the medium-power lens is in place.

3. Look through the eyepiece. If what you're looking at is not clear enough, slowly turn the adjusting knob to focus again.

4. Next, without moving the slide, rotate the nosepiece until the high-power objective lens is in place. You may need to move the adjusting knob a tiny bit to keep the lens from scraping the slide, but don't move it a lot.

5. Look through the eyepiece. If what you're looking at is not clear enough, slowly turn the adjusting knob to focus again.

6. When you're done looking at your slide, you'll want to remove it. To do this, rotate the nosepiece back to the low-power objective lens. Use the adjusting knob to slowly move the stage until there is a lot of space between the slide and the lens. Now you can safely and easily remove the slide.

LOOK AT A SLIDE

For this activity you will need

- an elementary microscope
- a prepared slide

Steps

1. With someone helping you, do each of the steps of looking at a slide.

    1. Starting with the low-power lens, look through the eyepiece and turn the adjusting knob until you can see the object clearly.
    2. Rotate the nosepiece until the medium-power lens is in place.
    3. Look through the eyepiece, and if the object is not clear, turn the adjusting knob to focus again.
    4. Rotate the nosepiece until the high-power lens is in place.
    5. Look through the eyepiece, and if the object is not clear, turn the adjusting knob to focus again.
    6. To remove the slide, rotate the nosepiece back to low power. Use the adjusting knob until there is a lot of space between the slide and lens, and remove the slide.

2. Practice doing the steps over and over until you can easily focus the microscope, change from one power to another, and correctly remove the slide.

7

You can make your own slides to look at things you are interested in.

First put a thin layer of what you want to look at on a slide. Microscopes shine a light from under the slide, so the layer must be thin enough for light to shine through it. You won't be able to see thick or very dark things well.

You might want to look at some bigger things, like dry powder, or a bug, without a cover slip.

When you look at something tiny, like a hair, place it on the slide, add a drop of water to the slide and cover it with a cover slip. The water will help keep the cover slip from moving around.

When you want to look at a liquid, just put a drop of it on a slide and cover it with a cover slip.

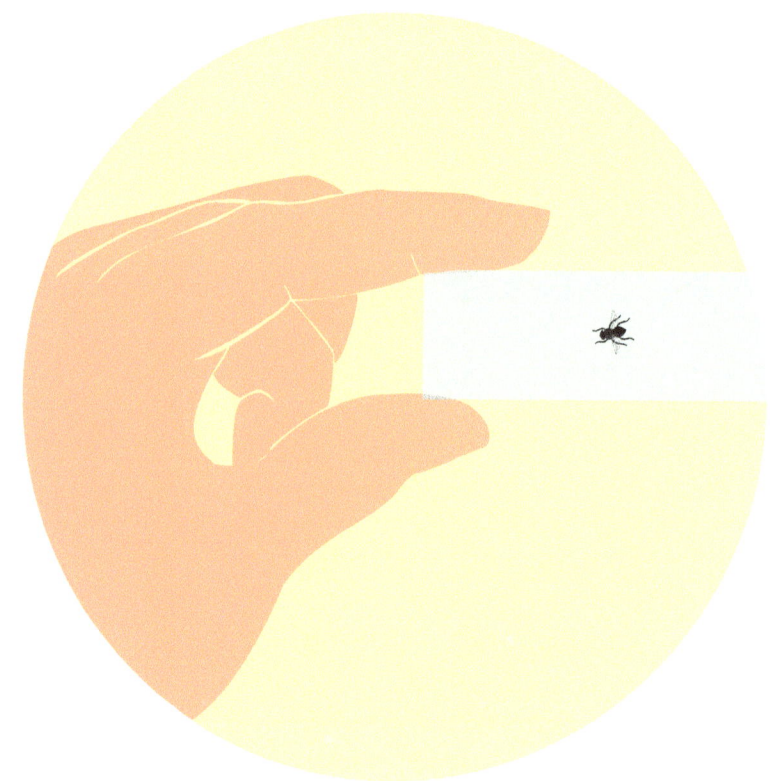

MAKE YOUR OWN SLIDE

For this activity you will need

- an elementary microscope
- a slide and cover slip
- a hair

Steps

1. Put a hair on your slide.
2. Add a drop of water and cover it with a cover slip.
3. Set up your microscope using your new slide.
4. Focus your microscope to give you the best look at your slide.
5. Have another person look at your slide.

8

Scientists learn more about things by looking at them.

When you look at something with a microscope, drawing what you see can be helpful. Why?

When you are asked to draw exactly what you see, it helps you LOOK even more closely.

Drawing something carefully also helps you remember what it looked like.

Another use of drawing is to show others what you have seen.

There are different ways to look and draw. Some people keep both eyes open when they are looking through the microscope. This way they can look with one eye and draw with the other at the same time.

Some people keep one eye closed when looking through the microscope. They look and then draw, then look again and draw some more.

Use the way that works best for you!

low power

leaf

medium power

leaf

high power

leaf

DRAW POWDER

For this activity you will need

- an elementary microscope
- a slide
- talcum (baby) powder

Steps

1. In your science journal, use a glass or jar lid to trace three circles, each about 3 inches wide.

2. Label your circles "talcum powder low", "talcum powder medium", and "talcum powder high".

3. Put a very tiny bit of talcum powder on a slide. Do not put a cover slip on it.

4. Set up your microscope using your slide.

5. Look at the edge of the powder.

6. Draw what you see using all three powers.

7. Share your drawings with someone, and tell them which power you think worked the best.

DRAW SALT

For this activity you will need

- an elementary microscope
- a slide
- table salt

Steps

1. In your science journal, use a glass or jar lid to trace three circles, each about 3 inches wide.

2. Label your circles "table salt low", "table salt medium", and "table salt high".

3. Put a very tiny bit of salt on a slide. Do not put a cover slip on it.

4. Set up your microscope using your slide.

5. Look at the salt.

6. Draw what you see using all three powers.

7. Share your drawings with someone, and tell them which power worked the best.

DRAW SUGAR

For this activity you will need

- an elementary microscope
- a slide
- sugar

Steps

1. In your science journal, use a glass or jar lid to trace three circles, each about 3 inches wide.

2. Label your circles "sugar low", "sugar medium", and "sugar high".

3. Put a very tiny bit of sugar on a slide. Do not put a cover slip on it.

4. Set up your microscope using your slide.

5. Look at the sugar.

6. Draw what you see using all three powers.

7. Share your drawings with someone, and tell them which power worked the best.

DRAW ONION SKIN

For this activity you will need

- an elementary microscope
- prepared slide of onion skin

Steps

1. In your science journal, use a glass or jar lid to trace three circles, each about 3 inches wide.

2. Label your circles "onion skin low", "onion skin medium", and "onion skin high".

3. Set up your microscope using your prepared slide.

4. Look at the onion skin.

5. Draw what you see using all three powers.

6. Share your drawings with someone, and tell them which power worked the best.

DRAW A BUG

For this activity you will need

- an elementary microscope
- a slide and cover slip
- tiny bug or parts of a bug (or a prepared slide of a bug)

Steps

1. In your science journal, use a glass or jar lid to trace three circles, each about 3 inches wide.

2. Label your circles "bug low", "bug medium", and "bug high".

3. If you don't have a prepared slide of a bug, find a tiny bug or parts of a bug, and squash it with a cover slip.

4. Set up your microscope using your slide.

5. Look at the bug.

6. Draw what you see using all three powers.

7. Share your drawings with someone, and tell them which power worked the best.

DRAW A FEATHER

For this activity you will need

- an elementary microscope
- prepared slide of a feather

Steps

1. In your science journal, use a glass or jar lid to trace three circles, each about 3 inches wide.

2. Label your circles "feather low", "feather medium", and "feather high".

3. Set up your microscope using your prepared slide.

4. Look at the feather.

5. Draw what you see using all three powers.

6. Share your drawings with someone, and tell them which power worked the best.

DRAW A BUG WITH WINGS

For this activity you will need

- an elementary microscope
- prepared slide of a squashed gnat or other tiny bug with wings

Steps

1. In your science journal, use a glass or jar lid to trace a circle about 3 inches wide. Label your circle "bug with wings".
2. Set up your microscope using your prepared slide.
3. Look at the bug.
4. Choose the power you think works best.
5. Draw part of a wing in the circle. Underneath, write what power you used.
6. Share your drawing with someone.

DRAW POND WATER

For this activity you will need

- an elementary microscope
- a slide and cover slip
- dirty water from a pond or puddle.

Steps

1. In your science notebook, use a glass or jar lid to trace a circle about 3 inches wide. Label your circle "dirty pond water".

2. Put a drop of dirty pond water on a slide and cover it with a cover slip.

3. Set up your microscope using your slide.

4. Look at the water.

5. Choose the power you think works best.

6. Draw what you see.

7. Share your drawing with someone.

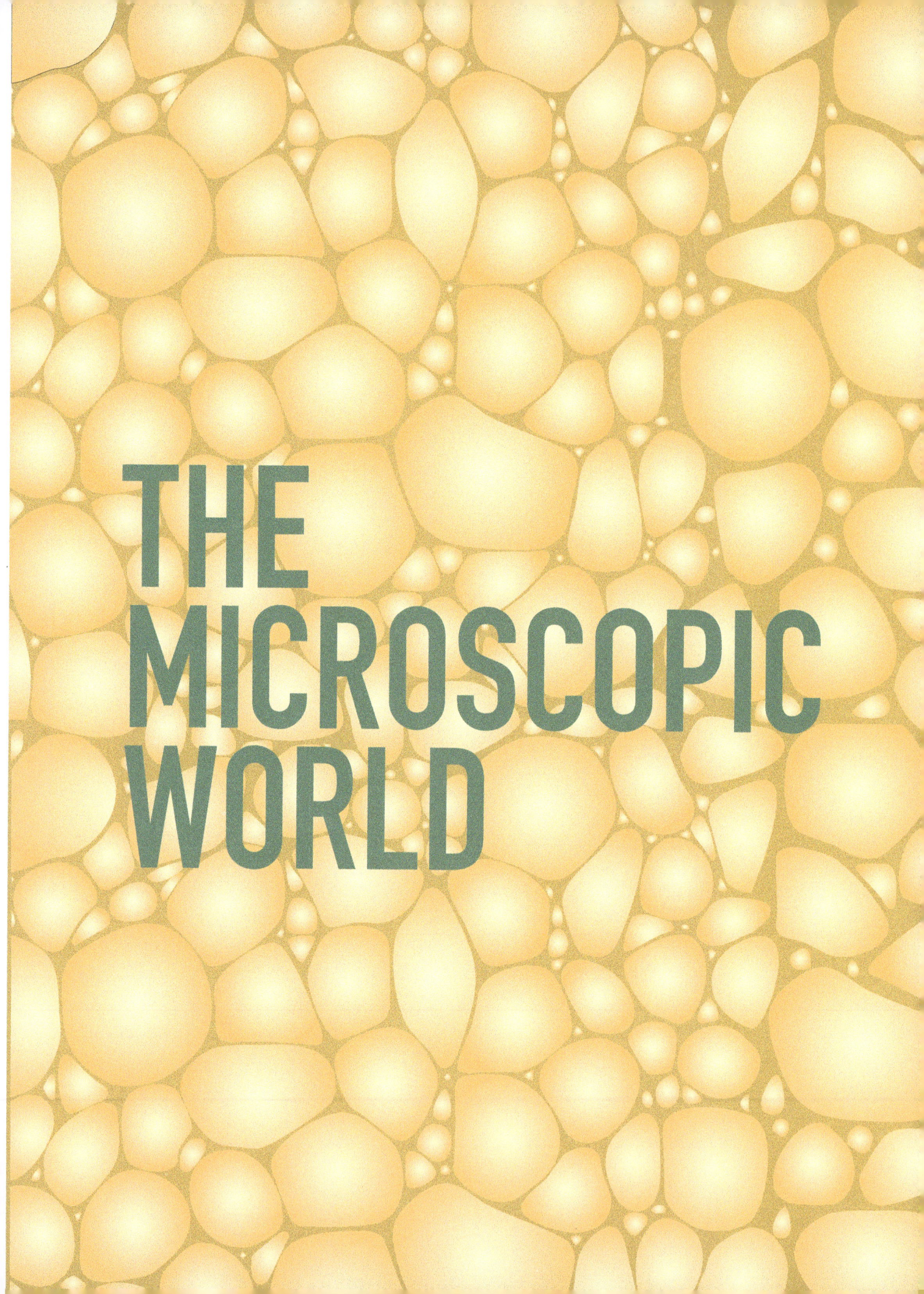

THE MICROSCOPIC WORLD

9

Something that is **microscopic** is so small you need a microscope to see it.

cloth

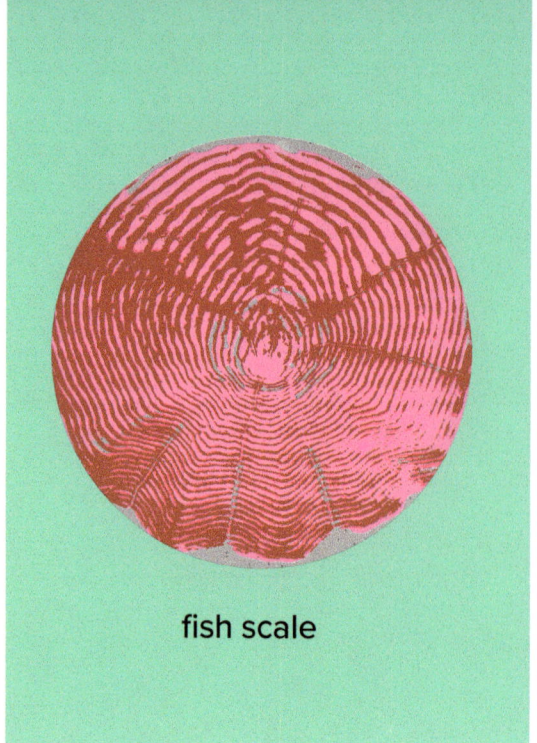
fish scale

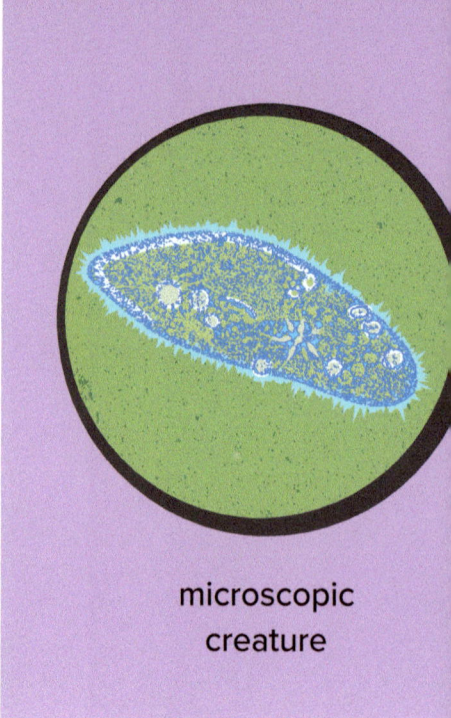
microscopic creature

Learning to use a microscope opens up a whole new world of tiny things you have never been able to see before. This is called the microscopic world!

The microscopic world is all around us.

By looking at the microscopic world, you can understand the things around you in a whole new way.

What other amazing things are there to discover in the microscopic world?

You're a young scientist.
Go find out!

DRAW A NEW OBJECT

For this activity you will need

- an elementary microscope
- a slide (and cover slip if needed)
- a new object of your choice

Steps

1. In your science journal, use a glass or jar to trace a circle about 3 inches wide. Label your circle.
2. Get your slide ready with your object. Use a cover slip, if needed.
3. Set up your microscope using your slide.
4. Look at your object.
5. Choose the power you think works best.
6. Draw what you see.
7. Share your drawing with someone.

www.ingramcontent.com/pod-product-compliance
Lightning Source LLC
Chambersburg PA
CBHW040312240426
43666CB00026B/2938